KEEP CALM
AND
LOVE
PIGS

Lightly ruled pages for reminders, journaling, and note taking.

A Notebook and Journal for Creativity and Mindfulness

© 2017 RW Squared Media
All Rights Reserved

ISBN-13: 978-1542395441

ISBN-10: 1542395445

RWSquaredMedia.Wordpress.com

Dogs look up to us. Cats look down on us.
Pigs treat us as equals.

Pigs are not that dirty. And they're smart, strange little creatures. They just need love.

Don't give cherries to pigs, or advice to fools.

Pigs are smarter than dogs, and both are smarter than Congress.

Dogs look up to us. Cats look down on us.
Pigs treat us as equals.

Pigs are not that dirty. And they're smart, strange little creatures. They just need love.

Don't give cherries to pigs, or advice to fools.

Pigs are smarter than dogs, and both are smarter than Congress.

Dogs look up to us. Cats look down on us.
Pigs treat us as equals.

Pigs are not that dirty. And they're smart, strange little creatures. They just need love.

Don't give cherries to pigs, or advice to fools.

Pigs are smarter than dogs, and both are smarter than Congress.

Dogs look up to us. Cats look down on us.
Pigs treat us as equals.

Pigs are not that dirty. And they're smart, strange little creatures. They just need love.

Don't give cherries to pigs, or advice to fools.

Pigs are smarter than dogs, and both are smarter than Congress.

Dogs look up to us. Cats look down on us.
Pigs treat us as equals.

Pigs are not that dirty. And they're smart, strange little creatures. They just need love.

Don't give cherries to pigs, or advice to fools.

Pigs are smarter than dogs, and both are smarter than Congress.

Dogs look up to us. Cats look down on us.
Pigs treat us as equals.

Pigs are not that dirty. And they're smart, strange little creatures. They just need love.

Don't give cherries to pigs, or advice to fools.

Pigs are smarter than dogs, and both are smarter than Congress.

Dogs look up to us. Cats look down on us.
Pigs treat us as equals.

Pigs are not that dirty. And they're smart, strange little creatures. They just need love.

Don't give cherries to pigs, or advice to fools.

Pigs are smarter than dogs, and both are smarter than Congress.

Dogs look up to us. Cats look down on us.
Pigs treat us as equals.

Pigs are not that dirty. And they're smart, strange little creatures. They just need love.

Don't give cherries to pigs, or advice to fools.

Pigs are smarter than dogs, and both are smarter than Congress.

Dogs look up to us. Cats look down on us.
Pigs treat us as equals.

> Pigs are not that dirty. And they're smart, strange little creatures. They just need love.

Don't give cherries to pigs, or advice to fools.

Pigs are smarter than dogs, and both are smarter than Congress.

Dogs look up to us. Cats look down on us.
Pigs treat us as equals.

Pigs are not that dirty. And they're smart, strange little creatures. They just need love.

Don't give cherries to pigs, or advice to fools.

Pigs are smarter than dogs, and both are smarter than Congress.

Dogs look up to us. Cats look down on us. Pigs treat us as equals.

Pigs are not that dirty. And they're smart, strange little creatures. They just need love.

Don't give cherries to pigs, or advice to fools.

Pigs are smarter than dogs, and both are smarter than Congress.

Dogs look up to us. Cats look down on us.
Pigs treat us as equals.

Pigs are not that dirty. And they're smart, strange little creatures. They just need love.

Don't give cherries to pigs, or advice to fools.

Pigs are smarter than dogs, and both are smarter than Congress.

Dogs look up to us. Cats look down on us.
Pigs treat us as equals.

Pigs are not that dirty. And they're smart, strange little creatures. They just need love.

Don't give cherries to pigs, or advice to fools.

Pigs are smarter than dogs, and both are smarter than Congress.

Dogs look up to us. Cats look down on us.
Pigs treat us as equals.

Pigs are not that dirty. And they're smart, strange little creatures. They just need love.

Don't give cherries to pigs, or advice to fools.

Pigs are smarter than dogs, and both are smarter than Congress.

Dogs look up to us. Cats look down on us.
Pigs treat us as equals.

Pigs are not that dirty. And they're smart, strange little creatures. They just need love.

Don't give cherries to pigs, or advice to fools.

Pigs are smarter than dogs, and both are smarter than Congress.

Dogs look up to us. Cats look down on us.
Pigs treat us as equals.

> Pigs are not that dirty. And they're smart, strange little creatures. They just need love.

Don't give cherries to pigs, or advice to fools.

Pigs are smarter than dogs, and both are smarter than Congress.

Dogs look up to us. Cats look down on us.
Pigs treat us as equals.

Pigs are not that dirty. And they're smart, strange little creatures. They just need love.

Don't give cherries to pigs, or advice to fools.

Pigs are smarter than dogs, and both are smarter than Congress.

Dogs look up to us. Cats look down on us.
Pigs treat us as equals.

Pigs are not that dirty. And they're smart, strange little creatures. They just need love.

Don't give cherries to pigs, or advice to fools.

Pigs are smarter than dogs, and both are smarter than Congress.

Dogs look up to us. Cats look down on us.
Pigs treat us as equals.

Pigs are not that dirty. And they're smart, strange little creatures. They just need love.

Don't give cherries to pigs, or advice to fools.

Pigs are smarter than dogs, and both are smarter than Congress.

Dogs look up to us. Cats look down on us.
Pigs treat us as equals.

Pigs are not that dirty. And they're smart, strange little creatures. They just need love.

Don't give cherries to pigs, or advice to fools.

Pigs are smarter than dogs, and both are smarter than Congress.

Dogs look up to us. Cats look down on us.
Pigs treat us as equals.

> Pigs are not that dirty. And they're smart, strange little creatures. They just need love.

Don't give cherries to pigs, or advice to fools.

Pigs are smarter than dogs, and both are smarter than Congress.

Dogs look up to us. Cats look down on us.
Pigs treat us as equals.

Pigs are not that dirty. And they're smart, strange little creatures. They just need love.

Don't give cherries to pigs, or advice to fools.

Pigs are smarter than dogs, and both are smarter than Congress.

Dogs look up to us. Cats look down on us.
Pigs treat us as equals.

Pigs are not that dirty. And they're smart, strange little creatures. They just need love.

Don't give cherries to pigs, or advice to fools.

Pigs are smarter than dogs, and both are smarter than Congress.

Dogs look up to us. Cats look down on us.
Pigs treat us as equals.

Pigs are not that dirty. And they're smart, strange little creatures. They just need love.

Don't give cherries to pigs, or advice to fools.

Pigs are smarter than dogs, and both are smarter than Congress.

Dogs look up to us. Cats look down on us.
Pigs treat us as equals.

Pigs are not that dirty. And they're smart, strange little creatures. They just need love.

Don't give cherries to pigs, or advice to fools.

Pigs are smarter than dogs, and both are smarter than Congress.

Dogs look up to us. Cats look down on us.
Pigs treat us as equals.

Pigs are not that dirty. And they're smart, strange little creatures. They just need love.

Don't give cherries to pigs, or advice to fools.

Pigs are smarter than dogs, and both are smarter than Congress.

For more amazing journals and adult colouring books from RW Squared Media, visit:

Amazon.com
CreateSpace.com
RWSquaredMedia.Wordpress.com

She Believed She Could
So She Did Adult Coloring Book

Life Isn't About Waiting for the Storm to Pass, It's About Learning to Dance in the Rain

The Matryoshka Nesting Doll Coloring Book for Adults

Start Where You Are Adult Coloring Book

Made in the USA
Middletown, DE
21 December 2017